Leading Multicultural Teams:
The First Five Tools for Global Leaders

LEADING MULTICULTURAL TEAMS

The First Five Tools For Global Leaders

Andrew Hoskins

Rick Mann, PhD

Leading Multicultural Teams: The First Five Tools for Global Leaders
By Andrew Hoskins and Rick Mann, PhD

Published by: Clarion International, Colorado Springs, CO

www.ClarionStrategy.com
www.ClarionToolBox.com

Dedication
To the next generation of global leaders
as you seek to create clarity out of chaos.

Table of Contents

 **Clarion**ToolBox Series

Strategic Leaders Are Made, Not Born: The First Five Tools for Escaping the Tactical Tsunami by Rick Mann, PhD

Building Strategic Organizations: The First Five Tools of Strategy and Strategic Planning by Rick Mann, PhD

Strategic Finance for Strategic Leaders: The First Five Tools by Rick Mann, PhD and David Tarrant, MBA

Coaching: The First Five Tools for Strategic Leaders by Rick Mann, PhD

Enterprise Leaders: The First Five FIELD Tools by Rick Mann, PhD and Dean Diehl, EdD

Acknowledgments

Special thanks to the strategic leaders from Afghanistan, Australia, Belgium, Brazil, Canada, Central Asia, Colombia, DRC, Ethiopia, France, Germany, Ghana, Guatemala, Haiti, Hong Kong, India, Italy, Kenya, Korea, Lebanon, Liberia, Mali, Netherlands, New Zealand, Niger, Nigeria, Norway, Philippines, South Sudan, Sudan, Spain, Switzerland, Syria, Taiwan, Thailand, Tunisia, Turkey, UK, Uganda, USA, and Zimbabwe we have had the privilege of working with. As leaders and teammates, each of you provided a unique perspective.

Thanks to the skilled contributions and hard work from our series editor, Kara de Carvalho, and our series designer, Lieve Maas.

We also want to thank Faith (Andrew's wife) and Cheri (Rick's wife) for their enduring support through this project.

PREFACE

NOTE: This book is written mainly in Andrew's voice. If text is directly attributable to Rick, it will be noted.

My first extended cross-cultural experience was joining the Peace Corps. The US government sent me to Niger, West Africa. Niger is a former French colony, but I couldn't speak French, let alone Zarma or Tamashek, the two local dialects in the area where I would spend two years volunteering. Nearly everything about Niger was the polar opposite of all I had known growing up on a farm in the American Midwest.

I took it all in enthusiastically, learning the languages, eating the food, and changing my wardrobe. I even bought a camel for transportation. Yet, the harder I tried to integrate with this new culture, the more glaring the differences became. Curiosity and determination could not erase the stark dissimilarities that separated me from my new friends.

I remember feeling down one evening after an incident where I had unknowingly made it evident that I was not from around there. It was not the first time I had been laughed at, and it was funny, but I let it get to me this time.

Ishmael, a good friend, noticed my demeanor and came to sit with me. He listened to me complain, then said, "Andrew, we like you because you are different from us."

That was the first of many times that I would be reminded of culture's fascinating ability to reveal human differences and commonalities. Those two years of drinking tea with Tuaregs in the Sahara Desert set me on a life-long journey to understand cultural differences.

From Chaos to Clarity

Why am I writing this book? There are many with far more experience in leading multicultural teams. While I am not a culture expert, I have dedicated the past two decades to cross-cultural leadership. Together, Rick and I have led multicultural teams from every corner of the globe. We are deeply passionate about seeing multicultural teams succeed, and that is why we are writing this book.

This book is designed for leaders and their teams. You may want to get copies for your team and discuss it over a meal, hold a retreat, or read it together slowly, one chapter per month. However you use it, we hope it facilitates your team's continuous journey from chaos to clarity.

As part of the ClarionToolBox Series, this book:

- Can be read in an evening or on a weekend
- Summarizes the material of thought leaders to be more accessible
- Provides practical application of each new concept

Introduction

Thirty minutes into our monthly global leaders' meeting, I looked at the faces around the table and on the screen and thought, what a crazy combination of cultures—such a diverse group, but somehow it worked. To experience a strong connection to people so different from me; four continents and seven distinct cultures coming together with the clarity of purpose. What an incredible thing to be a part of.

The Potential Rewards

The most enriching experiences in life come when we broaden our perspective—when we learn to see things differently. A high-performing, multicultural team is one of the most exciting things I've had the privilege to be a part of. Little compares with the feeling one gets when participating in a cohesive, effective, culturally diverse team.

Sure, there are frustrations, but a multicultural team can be exhilarating if led well. This book aims to give you the tools to minimize frustration and maximize exhilaration.

When we challenge our deepest held
assumptions about the world,
we get mind-blowing results.

Cross-cultural encounters have a particular way of jolting us out of our comfort zone. Culture exists at a subconscious level. It is the stuff we get defensive about even when we don't know why.

When teammates challenge our deepest held assumptions about the world in a healthy way, we get mind-blowing results. Multicultural teams can have higher levels of innovation, more extraordinary problem-solving skills, and more frequent "A-ha" moments than single-culture teams. Their very composition can be an incubator for out-of-the-box thinking.

The Inherent Challenges

If you picked up this book, you might already know how enriching it can be to work with people from different cultures. But that means you also know how frustrating it can be. The opening quotation of this introduction could just as easily have been written this way.

> Thirty minutes into our monthly global leaders' meeting, I looked at the faces around the table and on the screen and thought, what a mess! We are speaking English, but it may as well be different languages. It is never clear what is being communicated. We take forever to reach an agreement, and I later find out that some still disagree after making a decision. I'm not sure we even have the same goal. This is chaos.

There is no doubt that multicultural teams require extra effort. Are they worth it? Our answer is a resounding "yes," and we hope you will agree with us by the end of this book. The most worthwhile ventures in life always require hard work. But rewards are waiting for anyone willing to put in the effort.

Who Should Read This Book?

Multicultural teams are becoming the norm in nearly all organizations regardless of the sector—for-profit or nonprofit, public or private. The skills needed to lead multicultural teams are in demand now, and the need is increasing.

This book is for you whether you are a team leader or a team member; whether your team is multicultural today or it will be soon; and whether your organization is already a mixture of cultures or you are just starting the journey.

This book provides tools for ex-pats or international workers living outside of their home country and those with whom they work. It can also be used by leaders who travel internationally frequently or by those who never leave their home country but regularly interact with other cultures at conferences or virtual meetings.

This book is a primer for leading multicultural teams from chaos to clarity. Whether your team is newly formed, long-established, or yet to be appointed, this book can help take your cross-cultural leadership to the next level.

The First Five Tools Overview

Leading cross-culturally requires a specific skill set. This book presents the first five tools of that skill set. The tools build on each other sequentially, so even if you feel you've mastered one of the earlier tools, we recommend taking them one by one and improving even further. Each chapter presents a different tool that addresses a challenge inherent in leading multicultural teams.

Challenge	Tool	Reward
Misunderstanding	Cultural awareness	Mutual respect
Feelings of superiority	Leveraging differences	Innovation
Ambiguity	Forming a team culture	Team cohesion
Defensiveness and blaming	Resolving conflict	Healthy debate
Ethnocentrism	Intercultural climate	Organizational transformation

When leading a multicultural team, some days will feel chaotic and others clear. We hope that this book helps you reduce the chaos and gives you the resources to move your team toward greater clarity. The goal is progress, not perfection.

DEFINING OUR TERMS

If our aim is greater team clarity, let's start by being clear on the words we use in this book.

Global Leaders

Are you a global leader? Leadership is about influence; it is not limited to a specific position or title. Whether or not you are your team's official leader, you have an opportunity to influence and lead. Global leaders can be found at all levels of an organization, both with and without formal authority. Every organization needs more global leaders.

For more on strategic leadership and developing strategic leaders within your organization, we highly recommend you read the first book in the ClarionToolBox Series, *Strategic Leaders Are Made, Not Born: The First Five Tools for Escaping the Tactical Tsunami.*

The ClarionToolBox Series was designed to make foundational leadership concepts accessible and practical. Below is a summary of the first five tools in *Strategic Leaders Are Made, Not Born.*

Creating Value What do you provide that others value?	Every endeavor is about creating value for others. Each member is expected to contribute value to the team and add value to the organization.
Self-Awareness How are you unique?	A leader must understand their strengths and weaknesses—how you see yourself and how others experience you.
Stakeholder Analysis Whom do you serve?	Map the individuals and groups most invested in what you do—at home, at work, and in your community. Different stakeholders have different needs.
Strategic Altitude At what altitude do you lead?	**Highest (Vision):** Where is my team going? **Middle (Strategy):** How can we get there? **Lowest (Tactical):** What needs to be done? What can you do to raise the level of your team's thinking?
Good-to-Great Rubric Are you getting better?	A leader must have a way to evaluate progress—a simple scale to measure what matters.

Growth Mindset

We believe that global leaders are made, not born. Leadership requires practice and discipline. We never arrive but are continuously improving. This attitude is known as a growth mindset. Psychologist and Stanford professor Carol Dweck coined the term to describe the belief that one can improve any skill with deliberate effort. She contrasts this with a fixed mindset, the belief that we are born with a particular set of talents. We all oscillate between these two mindsets, but the more we adopt a growth mindset, the more successful we will be.

Leading multicultural teams is a skill you can learn. Armed with the tools in this book and deliberate effort, you can improve. As you see progress, your team will notice the difference. We hope that this book sets you on a lifelong journey in global leadership.

High-Performance Teams

A team is made up of individuals, each with unique strengths and weaknesses. However, high performance comes from how a group works together, not from the individuals that make up the team. The magical thing about teams is that they can be greater than the sum of their parts. High-performance teams intentionally evaluate how they function as a group; they regularly pull back the curtain to assess how they do what they do.

You must first understand team leadership before adding the multicultural dimension. A team leader who understands high-performing teams but is clueless about culture will outperform a culture expert who is a poor leader. First, know what it takes to achieve team performance, then add the complexity of culture.

See Appendix A for a quick refresher on managing high-performance teams.

Multicultural Teams

What do we mean by "multicultural" or "intercultural?" We use these terms interchangeably in this book. In short, we are talking about teams made up of people from different nationalities. Culture is always about a group not an individual. A culture describes people with a shared history and shared beliefs and values. While personality describes how an individual thinks and interacts with others, culture describes the common ways people in one geographical location believe and interact with others. To keep it simple, in this book, when we talk about culture, we are talking about nation of origin.

While nationality is certainly not the only way to define culture, it is significant. Even with an increase in globalization, countries remain the simplest and most effective way to evaluate differences between groups of people worldwide. National culture affects people's identities, unconscious value systems, behaviors, and motivations.

Geert Hofstede (2005) describes culture as a person's mental programming—the operating system by which all experiences are understood. While the manifestations of culture are visible, cultural values are underneath the surface. These national cultural values, the invisible aspects of culture, can create confusion and miscommunication among team members.

Culture Is Just One Aspect of Diversity

People differ in many ways: education, ethnicity, race, personality, gender, socioeconomic class, and more. You can apply the leadership principles in this book to teams with other forms of diversity, but the tools we discuss here are specifically designed for teams that are diverse because their members hail from different nations. We recommend reading Rohini Anand's (2021) book *Leading Global Diversity, Equity, and Inclusion* to learn more about broad diversity within multicultural teams.

CURRENT THOUGHT LEADERS

Part of the value of this book, and all those in the ClarionToolBox Series, is that it incorporates key insights from thought and practice leaders around this topic. This book summarizes thousands of pages of their well-known works. A few of these include:

- Erin Meyer. (2014). *The Culture Map: Breaking Through the Invisible Boundaries of Global Business*
- Geert Hofstede, Gert Jan Hofstede, and Michael Minkov. (2005). *Cultures and Organizations: Software of the Mind*
- Philippe Rosinski. (2003). *Coaching Across Cultures: New Tools for Leveraging National, Corporate & Professional Differences*
- Patrick Lencioni. (2012). *The Advantage: Why Organizational Health Trumps Everything Else in Business*
- Amy C. Edmonson. (2012). *Teaming: How Organizations Learn, Innovate, and Compete in the Knowledge Economy*

- Timothy R. Clark. (2020). *The 4 Stages of Psychological Safety: Defining the Path to Inclusion and Innovation*

NOTE: All these authors and titles can be found in the book's reference section at the end.

THE WHY, HOW, AND WHAT FRAMEWORK

As with other books in the ClarionToolBox Series, each chapter follows the same outline: why, how, and what.

- **WHY** It Matters – We explain the benefits of the tool and the risks if it is absent.
- **HOW** It Works – We unpack the essential concepts with clear examples.
- **WHAT** To Do Next? – We suggest practical ways to apply the tool to your leadership and then teach it to your team.

This simple "why, how, and what" framework will help you absorb the concepts quickly and apply each tool so that you can lead multicultural teams effectively.

1.

CULTURAL AWARENESS

Growing Mutual Respect

Sometimes you have to step out of the water
to realize you are wet.

As a boy, my father took me fishing. I remember imagining what it would be like to be a fish. Does a fish understand the concept of water when being wet is all it knows? I concluded that a fish probably has no notion of being wet because it has never been dry. It would have to come out of the water to truly comprehend wetness.

We are the same when it comes to our own culture. We can learn about cultural differences, but we don't really understand them until we step out of our culture and interact with those different from us. We only gain cultural awareness through lived experience.

Gaining Cultural Clarity

Culture affects the very core of who we are, what we believe, and how we behave. It is our mental programming operating in the background. Culture describes how we think rather than what we think about. It lies so deep within us that it usually goes unnoticed. Culture is what we assume to be universally true, often without realizing that not everyone agrees with our assumptions.

People from the same culture generally agree on things like what makes a good leader or what forms of communication are acceptable.

In a multicultural team, people's assumptions are different. Yet because these assumptions are unconscious, they cause misunderstanding. Even the most experienced cross-cultural leader can be caught off guard when a team members' actions contradict their deep cultural beliefs.

Most people live their entire lives oblivious to cultural differences. They ignore culture because they are surrounded by people who share the same assumptions. Culture only comes to the surface through encountering someone with different assumptions. A multicultural team generates these cross-cultural encounters.

Cultural encounters can either be a source of frustrating conflict or incredible creativity, depending on your cultural awareness level.

Beyond Handshakes and Head Nods

Cultural awareness is being attentive to our mental programming. It goes deeper than just noticing that handshakes and head nods differ from country to country. Leading multicultural teams requires moving beyond the surface-level aspects of culture. It is good, and even important, to learn greetings, appropriate body language, and what is polite or offensive in another culture. But these things alone are not enough.

The cultural awareness needed to lead a multicultural team demands more than reading a travel guide or attending a pre-departure briefing. Successful multicultural teams learn to interact at a deeper level. Teams that challenge each other's unconscious assumptions generate genuinely original ideas.

In order for awareness to take root in a team, a leader must humbly lead by example. The goal is for cultural encounters to be seen as learning experiences rather than a sequence of battles. The leader should model cultural curiosity and encourage individual team members to do the same. Eventually, curiosity will become part of the team culture.

*Successful multicultural teams
move beyond outward differences
to interact at a deeper level.*

No matter how much cross-cultural experience you have, humility is vital. There is a danger of dependency that can develop if your team views the leader as the cultural expert. A humble approach will diffuse defensiveness and create safety for the team. More on this in chapter 4.

Awareness is where it all starts—recognizing that you have a particular mental operating system because of where you grew up. This chapter lays the groundwork for helping you and your team understand yourselves.

WHY IT MATTERS

In today's shrinking world, leaders who can work effectively across cultures are in high demand. Organizations in nearly every sector are expanding their reach globally, requiring more people at all levels to interact cross-culturally. When global executives were asked to identify the most critical skill for success in today's environment, "the ability to influence people from other cultures" topped the list (Javidan, 2013, p. 506). Cultural awareness is a fundamental skill for today's strategic leaders.

Cultural awareness goes by different names: cultural intelligence, cultural aptitude, or interculturalism. At the core is the ability to navigate multiple cultures in a way that creates synergy. This synergy can create a high-performing, multicultural team that adds value to the organization.

Understanding cultural differences is **not the same as stereotyping.** I define culture as the common ways people think and interact with others. Cultures describe groups, not individuals. National cultures are, by definition, generalizations, so individuals will vary on how closely they identify with their culture's common assumptions and preferences. Some people will identify with more than one culture because of their lived experiences. For more on identifying with multiple cultures, see Appendix C.

---

*Cultural awareness does not replace the need
to get to know team members as individuals.*

National culture is only one part of a person's identity, but it is useful. Understanding national cultural preferences can help teams leverage differences and achieve high performance. Cultural awareness does not replace the need to get to know team members as individuals.

Never use culture as an excuse for labeling or pigeonholing others. Cultural awareness is about understanding, not excluding. If approached correctly, diversity can foster unity. Different cultural perspectives can drive innovation in your team.

HOW IT WORKS

So, how do we peek behind the curtain to examine our mental programming? Like a fish, how do we learn about the water we live in? We start by studying a different environment. We discover what is different among the world's various cultures, and then we assess how our culture compares.

Where do we fit on the spectrum from left to right? Cultures are multifaceted and can be sliced and diced many ways. I like to use Erin Meyer's eight cultural preferences with multicultural teams—eight ways to compare assumptions across countries. Some may argue that using eight different comparisons is too complex. Why not use three or five? There are simpler ways to compare cultures, but I feel these eight are particularly useful for multicultural teams. To better understand these eight comparisons, I highly recommend Myer's 2014 book, *The Culture Map*.

Understanding the extreme left and right
helps you assess where you fall on the line.

The table below lists Myer's eight cultural preferences down the middle. I explain the left and right sides of the spectrum for each preference. It is helpful to understand the two extremes for easy comparison, but most countries will fall somewhere in the middle. Reading examples of the extreme will help you assess your own culture's preferences.

	CULTURAL PREFERENCES	
Low-Context	COMMUNICATING	High-Context
Direct Feedback	EVALUATING	Indirect Feedback
Egalitarian	LEADING	Hierarchical
Consensus	DECIDING	Top-Down
Task-Based	TRUSTING	Relationship-Based
Confronting	DISAGREEING	Avoiding
Linear Time	SCHEDULING	Flexible Time
Principle-First	PERSUADING	Application-First

Communicating: Low-Context vs. High-Context

How do you prefer to communicate? Cultures vary in how they view good communication. In low-context communication, the communicator ensures that the message is clear. Communication is mainly through words, so what is said is paid attention to. Their goal is to minimize ambiguity. Low-context cultures like to repeat the main idea and summarize key takeaways after a meeting. The US and Canada are known for low-context communication.

Whereas low-context cultures place the burden of clarity on the communicator, high-context cultures expect more of the listener. High-context cultures value the listener's ability to decipher the message correctly. Their goal is to speak indirectly, expecting the listener to use context clues to understand the intended meaning. Communication happens by manipulating the context, doing something unexpected, for example. The actual message sent via the context may be the opposite of the words being said.

Summarizing bullet points or repeating key takeaways can come across as condescending in high-context cultures, as if the communicator does not think the listener can understand. In high-context communication, the communicator gives the listener dignity by not speaking too directly—treating the listener like an adult, not a child. Most Asian and African countries naturally use high-context communication.

Working in Uganda, I learned to adjust my definition of good communication. Meetings often end before I am 100% clear on the outcome, but everyone else understands perfectly. After the meeting, I would ask someone on my team to fill me in on the context—the value of a traditional saying or the significance of a story. Sometimes what was not said carried more weight than the words spoken.

In general, low-context communication should be the default within multicultural teams. High-context communication works only when everyone comes from the same context. For example, I have used low-context communication to present the ideas in this book. The chapter outlines (why, how, and what) are intentionally simple for clarity. My goal is for this book to be understood in multiple contexts.

Evaluating: Direct vs. Indirect

How do you give negative feedback? How do you prefer to receive negative feedback? Providing feedback on performance is critical in a work environment, and sometimes it will be negative. Cultures can be compared by how directly they prefer to give and receive negative feedback.

Remember, politeness is in the eye of the beholder. There is no universal understanding of 'nice.' What is polite in one culture may be rude in another.

The Netherlands is on the extreme left, preferring direct negative feedback. In cultures with this preference, it is respectful to point out areas for improvement in the most straightforward way possible. Just come out and say it; holding back does not help anyone.

In indirect cultures, giving negative feedback directly is rude. Cultures that prefer indirect negative feedback use a roundabout way of giving criticism, avoiding any chance of public shame. It is better to pull someone aside privately than risk losing face.

The US falls just slightly on the indirect side of the scale. From a young age, Americans are taught to make a feedback sandwich—to encase a criticism between two compliments. The saying, "If you can't say something nice, don't say anything at all," comes from an indirect culture.

I [Rick] worked with a national leader from the Netherlands. He would ask me if he could be "Dutch" for a few moments. I knew that whatever he said next was going to cut to the chase (and be negative). In contrast to this, when I [Rick] worked in Asia for many years, I had to learn how to be very indirect. Through these experiences, I learned that I needed to adapt my directness based on the preference and culture of that person.

Politeness is in the eye of the beholder.

You may have noted that these first two cultural comparisons deal with communication. The first describes context preferences, while the second is specific to negative evaluation. Both of these comparisons are important in a multicultural team because they can differ according to country. While most low-context countries also prefer direct negative feedback, there are exceptions. The U.S. uses low-context communication yet prefers indirect negative feedback.

Separate these two comparisons to understand how your team might prefer to communicate positive and negative messages differently. Do not assume that styles are the same for both types of messages; this could lead to miscommunication.

Leading: Egalitarian vs. Hierarchical

What is your idea of a good boss? How would you describe a great leader? Countries differ in how they answer these questions. Many leadership books try to make a case for universal characteristics of a good leader, but cultures differ in what they value. Countries prefer different types of authority figures.

Unfortunately, most books on leadership are written from a Western perspective. Multicultural teams must question assumptions presented as universal facts in leadership literature. Global leaders should encourage an open discussion about what makes a good leader.

Cultures can be either egalitarian or hierarchical. In the book *Cultures and Organizations*, Hofstede (2005) describes how power distance differs across cultures. An egalitarian culture has a low power distance, a small difference between organizational levels. Do you feel comfortable walking straight into the boss's office with a new idea? Egalitarian cultures value relative equality among team members and little separation between levels.

A hierarchical culture has a high-power distance, a large difference in power between organizational levels. Hierarchical cultures tend to have a separation between the boss and subordinates. You know your place and do not cross the line. Respecting the leader entails maintaining the distinction.

As a young leader working cross-culturally, I misunderstood the significance of this cultural preference. In an effort to show my team respect, I insisted on equality. I shunned anything that put me on a pedestal or visibly separated the leader from the team. In my culture, this was servant leadership, but it was confusing and sometimes embarrassing to my team. One day, I insisted on driving myself to a high-level meeting. While parking, I noticed that all the other attendees had been dropped off by their drivers. Only later did I realize that my actions conveyed shame, not respect.

Multicultural leaders who prefer egalitarian leadership should not dismiss hierarchical structures. The culturally aware leader understands there is no good or bad style. Each has their strengths.

Deciding: Consensus vs. Top-Down

How are decisions made: by consensus or a top-down decision? Cultures that prefer decision by consensus value harmony and unity. The decision process may take longer, but in the end, the entire team will be on board and ready to move forward. By obtaining 100% agreement, the implementation phase goes smoother. Unity facilitates collaborative action. These cultures are OK with putting in the long, tedious hours of reaching a decision that reflects a little bit of everyone involved. Once a decision is made, the hard work is mainly done.

On the other hand, top-down decisions are quick, but getting everyone on board for implementation takes time. Cultures that place a high value on decision efficiency do not mind letting one individual make the decision and then working to build buy-in later. The initial decision is quick, but the implementation phase is an iterative process of feedback and compromise.

Which do you value more:
harmony or efficiency?

With top-down decisions, the exact details of the decision can be tweaked during the team buy-in process. This is not true of consensus cultures. When evaluating your decision preference, ask yourself when you put in the hard work of building an agreement and negotiating a compromise. Is it before any decision is made, after, or somewhere in the middle?

The third and fourth scales are often related in our minds, similar to the first two. Sometimes leading and deciding are combined into one comparison. You might assume that hierarchical cultures would always prefer top-down decisions and that egalitarian cultures prefer consensus. While this is true for many, it is not valid for all.

The US and Canada are relatively egalitarian cultures that prefer top-down decision-making in many situations. Conversely, Germany is more hierarchical yet prefers consensus. I recommend that your team view these two comparisons separately to avoid misunderstanding.

Trusting: Task vs. Relationship

Do you approach work based on relationships or tasks? In cultures that emphasize task-based relationships, team trust is built by getting the job done. A team member's reliability gives the rest of the team confidence.

Task-based cultures will often clearly separate between personal life and work life. Do you consider it unethical to mix personal relationships with business? The US is an example of a task-based country that typically separates business and personal.

In relationship-oriented cultures, it is common to mix business and personal. Business is intentionally conducted using personal connections. Trust is built over time—much more time than in task-based cultures, but once forged, the relationship endures. Fewer, stronger ties are more important than multiple, superficial ones.

In relationship-based cultures, a quickly formed friendship is not a friendship at all, but a shallow acquaintance. When a personal relationship reaches a certain level of trust, only then is business discussed. India is one example of a culture that approaches trust through relationships rather than tasks.

I have been reminded of the importance of relationships numerous times. I was frustrated with Samesh, an Indian colleague who would not respond to my emails. He kept silent when I sent reminders about tasks with deadlines. It was beginning to affect his performance. After our first face-to-face meeting, I was able to observe Samesh for a full day. He was passionate about the work and clearly a high performer. This did not align with the assumptions I had made based on his lack of email communication. Over the evening meal, Samesh shared his own frustration with me. He considered my curt, task-focused emails rude. Was I not interested in his family? Could I not be bothered to ask about what was happening in his life outside of work?

That day we both realized how easy it was to make assumptions. Cultural awareness allows us to leverage both tasks and relationships for high performance. Disregarding either leads to misunderstanding.

Disagreeing: Confrontation vs. Avoiding

How do you disagree with someone? Do you dive in or dodge conflict to save face and maintain the relationship? Meyer (2014) describes cultures as either "confronting" or "avoiding."

Confronting cultures view conflict as productive and necessary. A good team has robust debates discussing the pros and cons of new ideas. Confrontation does not harm relationships; it strengthens them. It is a part of what a healthy team does. Israel and France are typical confronting cultures. They ask, "who's up for a good debate?"

Cultures on the avoiding side see disagreeing as damaging to relationships. They value group harmony, and openly debating an issue threatens the peace. Public confrontation brings shame. To save face, disagreements are dealt with privately, one-on-one, not in the open. Japan is a classic example of a country where conflict is often avoided.

Scheduling: Linear Time vs. Flexible Time

How do you view time? Different cultures view time on a spectrum from linear to flexible.

Anyone who has worked cross-culturally can tell a story of a scheduling miscommunication. While living in Liberia, I received a wedding invitation for10:00 am on a Saturday. I showed up, gift in hand, but was surprised to be the only one there. At noon other guests began to trickle in, but the ceremony didn't start until just after 2:00 pm. The family offered no excuses. Apparently, everyone but me knew that a 10 am invitation really meant 2 pm.

A cultural understanding of time explores the deep assumptions about its purpose. The words that a culture uses to describe time provide clues. A team that understands both ends of this scale will gain more than just knowing when to arrive for an invitation to be "on time."

Linear time depicts time as a line from the past to the future with a marker to indicate the present. The marker moves along this line in one direction and can never jump backward or forward. The present is the only time we have; it is a limited resource that must be "spent wisely" and "not wasted."

These cultures value promptness—if the meeting is at 10:00, arrive at 9:55 just to be safe. Tasks are completed sequentially with strict deadlines. Switzerland & Germany are both on the linear side of this comparison.

Flexible time, on the other hand, is seen as abundant. The present is not disconnected from the past or the future; it flows out from them. Time is a gift to be received, not a resource to be spent, so it cannot be "wasted." Time is the only thing we all have the same amount of every day, no matter one's social or economic status. Time is the great equalizer.

Flexible-time cultures value flexibility and adaptability. Deadlines are useful as goals but are not binding. Most African and Middle Eastern countries view time as flexible.

Persuading: Principles vs. Application

How do you persuade others of your ideas? If leadership is influence, the art of persuasion is critical. Yet, methods of convincing others vary by culture. Do you start from a theoretical perspective or jump straight to practical application?

Cultures that focus on application first when presenting a new idea are quick to list action steps. A report may begin with an executive summary that includes the final recommendations. A presentation may open with an overview of the key takeaways. The conclusion is often given first, explained, and then repeated at the end. Aristotle put it this way, "Tell them what you are going to tell them, tell them, and then tell them what you told them." The U.S. and Canada prefer this method of applications-first persuading.

Cultures that take a principle-first approach prefer to start with the underlying concepts that all can agree on. The emphasis is on explaining the methodology and reasoning before drawing any conclusion. Presentations systematically move from principle to principle, allowing the listener to draw conclusions.

If recommendations are given at all, they are presented as flowing out of a natural conclusion. Principle-first cultures value the foundational principles and want to convey the thought processes before any action steps are discussed. France is an example of a country that prefers principle-first persuasion.

If leadership is influence, how does your culture view the art of persuasion?

This book is written with an application-first persuasion style. Each chapter provides practical recommendations rather than leaving it up to the reader to decipher. Both authors come from an application-first culture, so this book only touches on underlying principles; they are not the central focus.

Eight Ways to Map Culture

The summary of these eight cultural comparisons comes from the research presented in Erin Meyer's book, *The Culture Map*. The keyword is 'comparison.' To gain awareness of our own cultures, we must compare it with others. Cultural awareness is not about judgment; it is about broadening our perspective.

Remember, culture is not about good or bad, right or wrong. Each of these perspectives adds something unique to the creative process. A competent global leader will leverage multiple cultural perspectives according to the situation at hand.

WHAT TO DO NEXT

Start with a self-assessment to see where you fall on each spectrum. Cultural preferences are just that, preferences, not constraints. You may be able to relate to both the left and right descriptions but ask yourself which one your culture as a whole prefers. Imagine what an average person would default to in a team setting.

If you have spent significant time in another culture, you may easily identify with multiple preferences, but the culture of your childhood is still likely the strongest; it will be your default reaction in times of stress. For more on this point, see Appendix C.

Mapping Your Culture

Reread the eight descriptions one at a time. Take out a piece of paper and draw a line for each. Plot where your culture falls on the line by asking the question, "What does my culture generally prefer?"

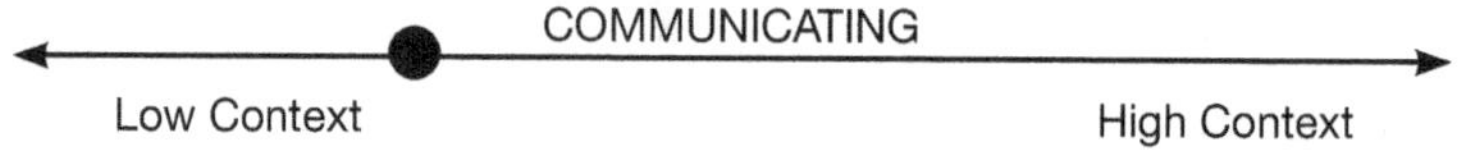

It is helpful to try and imagine how an average manager or employee would respond. Think about times when you have been defensive, reacted strongly, or shut down after a cultural encounter. Why did you react that way? Note the behaviors that you unconsciously favored or rewarded in your team. Your answers may provide clues to how culture influences your leadership.

Teach It to Your Team

Conduct a team assessment. Have your team read the descriptions of the eight preferences or present them briefly during one dedicated meeting. Give examples of the left and right extremes and allow time for questions to ensure that everyone understands the scales.

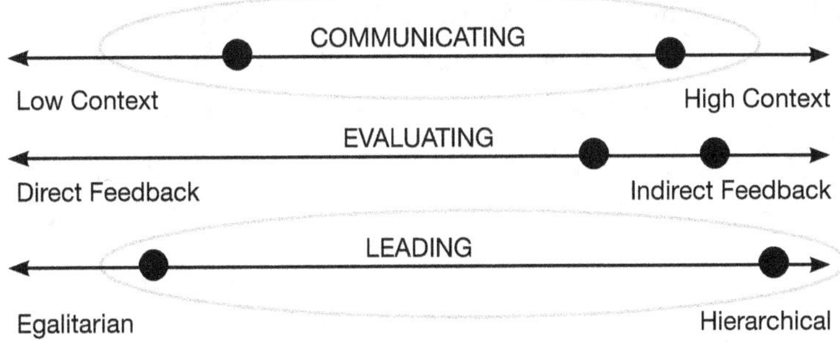

Now visually plot where each team member falls on the eight lines using colored sticky notes or something similar. Pay attention to the two or three most significant gaps between each culture. These gaps will vary between any two cultures, so the value of this exercise is to identify the most significant differences on the team. The differences are potential conflict points, but, as I will discuss in the next chapter, they can be leveraged as sources of innovation.

Cross-Cultural Immersion

Having a keen cultural awareness is increasingly necessary for today's strategic leaders. Because cultural preferences are unconscious, the natural tendency is to assume everyone thinks as we think. Cross-cultural immersion is one way to move past this tendency. Leaders who have spent a significant period of time in a different culture can more easily spot cultural differences. Immersion is the best way to hone this skill. I'm talking about more than short-term travel. Going about your daily routine in a completely different context opens your eyes and helps you see your own culture more clearly.

While leading a multicultural team produces cultural encounters, it is no replacement for the experience of relocating. If given the opportunity, regular physical interaction with a different culture is the best way to develop cultural awareness.

Express your interest in international opportunities in your organization, if they exist. Ask about the possibility of temporarily relocating to a country where your organization operates. Seek out international volunteer opportunities that would allow you to relocate for a minimum of six months. These types of experiences will make you stand out from the crowd.

2.

LEVERAGING DIFFERENCES

Increasing Innovation

Strength lies in differences, not in similarities.

–Stephen R. Covey

"Why don't you take him out for lunch?" my colleague, Okello, asked. I was confused by the question. I thought we were brainstorming how to move the project forward. We were talking about how to modify our proposal to meet the unreasonable demands of one particular government official. Now this team member was asking about lunch plans?

I started to bring the team back on task. And then I paused, realizing that this could be a cultural moment. In my culture, taking a government official to lunch would be inappropriate. But the project was not being implemented in my culture. We talked it through as a team and decided to invest in the relationship. Giving the official a chance to air his concerns privately proved vital to the project's success.

Differences are what make a team great. Teams that share all the same strengths and weaknesses fail. This chapter is about leveraging a team's diversity.

Humans have appreciated diversity from the beginning. We need people who are different from us. Our innate desire for community comes from a longing to be around others. And others are, by definition, not us. Specialization, division of labor, and even society itself are built on leveraging individuals' different strengths. The old take care of the young; the strong help the weak. The ability to leverage differences is a fundamental building block of human society. It is also a building block of human conflict, as we will see in the next chapter.

Cultural awareness highlights the fact that we are all different. Internalizing this concept is crucial because it moves us past our unconscious assumption that we are all the same. We need a balanced understanding of the existence of similarities and fundamental differences.

Some of our disagreements and conflicts have culture at their root. The first tool created awareness of the different assumptions that influence how we think and behave. This second tool allows us to leverage these differences as sources of creativity.

WHY IT MATTERS

Being aware of differences is a start, but it is not enough; multicultural teams cannot stop there. Teams must learn to embrace their differences and navigate between cultural perspectives depending on the situation. High-performing teams celebrate their disagreements because they know they are the source of their success.

---

*Teams generate ideas
that no individual can come up with alone.*

Marriage is a perfect example—a team of two. I fell in love with my wife because she was different from me. Her reactions to situations surprised me. Dating her was exciting; I was unpacking the mystery of who this woman was. She was definitely not the same as me.

Now that she is my wife, those same differences that I was so curious about when we were dating sometimes cause conflict. In the middle of an argument, I might say, "Why can't you just think like me?" In those moments, I am not intrigued by her uniqueness. I am frustrated that we can't agree.

When we are able to stop and reflect, my wife and I remind each other that we are a team. If we can understand each other's perspectives, we can leverage them both to create a unique solution. Whether the disagreement is about parenting, budgeting, or decorating the house, we have generated ideas that neither of us could have thought of alone.

Sometimes it helps to remind myself that I don't *want* my wife to agree with me all the time. After all, I fell in love with her because she was different from me.

---

*The team that masters the art of cultural reframing
has discovered a new superpower.*

The ability to leverage differences will transform your leadership. This chapter will show you how to first apply the concept to your own decision-making; how to then teach it to your team, and finally how to integrate it into your team culture.

You will learn to notice times when a new cultural perspective might be useful. You will begin regularly asking yourself the question, "Is there a cultural element to this situation?"

HOW IT WORKS

Start with any problem that needs solving or requires a decision. Consider the issue from different cultural angles. Many times, a fresh perspective provides an out-of-the-box solution. Reframing a question is a powerful problem-solving tool, and culture is the most significant frame that humans use unconsciously every day. The team that masters the art of cultural reframing has discovered a new superpower.

Yet, cultural adaptation is an individual process. Each person must take ownership of their own development. Incorporating this tool into your leadership will take time and deliberate practice. To get started, let's look at the five stages of cultural adaptation, taken from Philippe Rosinski's (2003) book *Coaching Across Cultures*.

Ignore	Recognize	Adapt	Integrate	Leverage

Stage 1: Ignore

The first stage is to ignore cultural differences. We are all born into this stage. Have you ever noticed how children act as if differences do not exist?

Multiple languages surrounded my oldest daughter from birth, so she was convinced she could speak any language she wanted at age three. I'll never forget her first interaction with a Chinese girl of her age. They both ran off to play, oblivious to the fact that they couldn't understand each other. Five minutes later, I heard my daughter "speaking" to her new friend with noises that, to her, sounded very Chinese. They were both using exaggerated hand gestures and getting their points across quite easily. Indeed, there seemed to be no language barrier between them, even though neither understood a single word.

Unfortunately, while ignorance may aid communication among children, it is a barrier in a team setting. At this first stage, team differences are dealt with at a surface level without ever realizing that there are various cultural assumptions at the root.

Stage 2: Recognize

The second stage is to recognize differences. Our eyes are opened to how culture causes people to think and behave differently. Mapping out where your team falls on each of the eight cultural scales from chapter one might open some eyes to individual cultural differences for the first time.

Notice how team members react when confronted with the different preferences rooted in culture. Recognition can cause three main reactions among team members. They can view the differences as negative, minimize them, or accept them. While there are three divergent paths within the recognition stage, only through accepting can one advance to the next stage, so watch out for the other two paths.

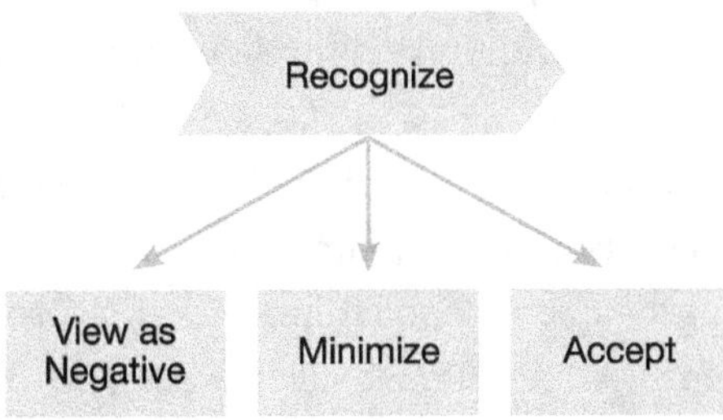

Viewing differences as negative is called ethnocentrism—the belief that your culture is better than others. People unconsciously believe that their way of doing things is superior. Teams that are dominated by one culture are more at risk of ethnocentrism. In these situations, the leader should watch out for hints of superiority.

Many organizations have one dominant culture due to where the organization started or where the head office is located. Ethnocentrism is often unknowingly built into structures and processes.

To move beyond the first phase of cultural recognition, you must openly discuss power dynamics within global organizations. Chapter five discusses this in more detail.

The second divergent path within this stage is to minimize the significance of differences. Minimizing is the opposite of ethnocentrism but is just as damaging to progress. Cultural differences are trivialized or glossed over.

One of the first multicultural teams that I led in Ethiopia comprised three very distinct national cultures. During times of conflict, my strategy was to downplay the significance of cultural differences. I reminded the team of our common goal and emphasized our similarities. I aimed to keep the peace, but it minimized the significant gaps in perspective from various cultures.

Leaders with extensive cross-cultural experience are prone to minimizing differences. Focusing on similarities alone prevents a leader from recognizing unique individual qualities. I shared a meal with a leader who spent his entire life outside his passport country. He had recently realized that his default leadership approach was to minimize cultural differences. He had mastered the first tool of cultural awareness and assumed that was enough. He hadn't progressed to the point of leveraging differences.

Minimizing is a sign that a team has not yet moved to the final path of recognition, accepting differences. Accepting cultural differences means that a team can acknowledge and appreciate each member's unique perspective. Acceptance implies more than just knowing that differences exist; team members begin to understand opposing views mutually.

Acceptance does not imply the surrender of one's own culture or an agreement by the team to adopt only one perspective. Accepting differences moves the group toward unity, not uniformity.

Stage 3: Adapt

Adaptation brings behavioral changes. Team members move outside their comfort zones and behave in ways that value other team members' preferences. The shifts in behavior may be temporary or specific to certain situations, but the teams functioning in this stage are acting out of cultural awareness.

One way adaptation shows up is in our speech. We learn to adjust the way we speak depending on who we are talking to. This is called code-switching, modifying our language to accommodate the listener. Code-switching exists even within different groups of native speakers. Just listen to a conversation among teenagers. Notice the words they use and the cadence of their speech. A teenager is able to immediately switch their speech patterns when addressing an adult.

We are not always aware of the different ways we try to adapt. While living in Liberia, I came home after a full day of straining to communicate in Liberian English. As I started speaking, my daughter stopped me and said, "Dad, just talk normally." She had noticed my exaggerated gestures and over pronunciation. I had been caught in a delayed code-switching mode. Speech and body language are noticeable ways we rapidly adapt between cultures.

Stage 4: Integrate

The fourth stage is integration—the ability to simultaneously hold conflicting cultural views in mind. I call this embracing the tension. In this stage, a team can evaluate situations through different cultural lenses.

Cultural perspectives are helpful frames of reference to see the problem from a different angle. Teams that reach cultural integration stop thinking in an "either-or" mindset and begin talking about "both-and."

Embracing the tension means the team can now view culture as another problem-solving tool. Rather than evaluating which culture is superior, the team can zoom out and view culture as one of the many perspectives that can be integrated into their decision-making.

Stage 5: Leverage

The final stage of cultural adaptation is leveraging differences. Teams that have reached this stage proactively leverage their unique combination of cultural perspectives in a way that maximizes creativity. Innovative ideas emerge by actively combining the thoughts and motivations of diverse team members. Leveraging creates synergy—the output is greater than the sum of the inputs.

Leveraging creates synergy—the output is greater than the sum of the inputs.

A team may reach this stage only momentarily or on a single project. The fleeting nature of synergy is part of its allure. Once your team experiences the flow of extremely high performance, you will want to achieve it again and again. Leveraging cultural differences can help you get into team flow more consistently.

Putting It All Together

This chapter has focused on adapting to differences. Teambuilding often highlights similarities, common ground, and a shared vision. While identifying commonalities is an essential part of the team formation process, it is not the end. Press forward and grow into a team that leverages your unique combination of cultural perspectives.

J.R.R. Tolkien's *Lord of the Rings* series tells the story of an unlikely team that forms around a common goal of destroying the ring of power. The Fellowship of the Ring is like a multicultural team, consisting of men, hobbits, a dwarf, an elf, and a wizard.

If you've read the books or watched the movies, you know that the Fellowship of the Ring suffers its share of cross-cultural conflict as they move through the stages of cultural adaptation. They are first ignorant of differences; some had never left their hometown. The group begins to recognize, adapt, and integrate their differences. The final battle scenes depict the Fellowship leveraging each member's strength. But the synergy is fleeting and does not last.

What other examples of the five stages of cultural adaptation from business, sports, or literature come to your mind? Stories are a great way to communicate this concept to your team.

Understanding Creativity

In the first tool, you learned to map the gap between cultural perspectives, identifying the two or three most significant gaps between each culture on your team. These gaps are now a list of the areas where your team has the greatest opportunity for leveraging. Simply referring to these differences as opportunities can positively impact your teamwork. Reframing our words is the first step to thinking differently.

It sounds simple, but reframing is powerful. When a team begins talking about cultural differences as leverage points rather than conflict points, they are on their way to achieving synergy.

When we feel stuck, it is often because we are viewing the problem from only one perspective.

Todd Henry (2013) is an author who dissects the creative process to demystify how we come up with ideas. He stresses the importance of using different modes of thinking when talking about a problem. When we feel stuck, it is often because we are viewing the problem from only one perspective. Changing our mode of thinking can lead to novel solutions. This is how creativity works. A team that hones the skill of leveraging perspectives will rise above repetition and produce fresh ideas.

WHAT TO DO NEXT

Cultural adaptation is a continuous process that requires intentionality. Assess where you are today, and ask what you can do to get to the next level. In certain contexts you may find that you are already at the leveraging stage, while in other contexts you ignore differences. Assess, reflect, then act; first yourself, then your team.

Apply It to You

For each stage, evaluate your leadership actions during the previous two weeks.

Stage	Self-evaluation
Ignore	How might I have ignored differences? Are there areas where I don't know what I don't know?
Recognize	What differences are annoying me? Have I minimized or trivialized? Have I openly appreciated someone's differences?
Adapt	When have I acted outside of my preferred style? (Communicating, Deciding, Leading, etc.)
Integrate	What tensions am I embracing? Am I able to hold contradictory perspectives?
Leverage	Am I using culture as a source of creativity? What innovative ideas have emerged?

One practical way to progress as a leader is to bring this process into the open. Talk about it out loud. Move beyond reading and internalizing. Try sharing these five stages with a friend and ask where they are. Ask them to evaluate where they think you are.

As your awareness increases, you will notice culture's relevance to more situations. Begin verbalizing this awareness. Start acknowledging the cultural element in conversations. Begin a one-on-one meeting by saying something like, "My natural style is to dive right into problem-solving, but I recognize the value of being more relational. So, how is your family doing?"

Simply acknowledging that culture is just a perspective is powerful. Unconsciously, our brains are constantly making assumptions. Talking about an assumption reminds us that it is an assumption, not a fact; it can be questioned. Regularly verbalizing your culture will unlock the ability to operate at the leverage stage.

Think of one or two people you will meet with this week to discuss these concepts. Better yet, form a group of peers outside your team to meet regularly and discuss things you are learning through leveraging cultures.

Teach It to Your Team

At which stage does your team operate? A team will consistently operate at the level of its least culturally adapted member. In other words, if one team member ignores differences, the entire team will be unable to progress beyond that stage of cultural adaptation. Therefore, it is critical to review these concepts as a team.

Stage	Person A	Person B	Person C	Person D
Leverage			X	
Integrate				
Adapt	X			
Recognize				X
Ignore		X		

Team operating level

Have your team read this chapter, or give them a summary and then facilitate a discussion using these questions.

1. Which stage best describes our team's normal operations?
2. What is an example of a time when we were ignorant of differences?
3. When have we leveraged differences?
4. How could we spend more time at the leveraging stage?

Combining the First Two Tools

Use the following questions as conversation starters to get your team thinking about leveraging differences. The left and right questions are arranged to highlight each end of the culture scale. Focus on the questions at the opposite end of where you or your team prefer to operate. For example, if I prefer low-context communication, I need to answer the question on the right side, "Can we encourage insider language to strengthen unspoken norms?"

CULTURE PULSE QUESTIONS		
Low-Context: Should we overcommunicate to ensure understanding?	**COMMUNICATING**	High-Context: Can we encourage insider language to strengthen unspoken norms?
Direct Feedback: Can we be more transparent about individual performance?	**EVALUATING**	Indirect Feedback: In what ways can we avoid shame and allow self-reflection?
Egalitarian: What do we appreciate about approachable leadership?	**LEADING**	Hierarchical: How can we clearly separate and clarify authority levels?

	DECIDING	
Consensus: When do we need to include more people in the decision?		Top-Down: What decisions are best decided by one person or a smaller group?
Task-Based: How can we make sure our personal interests do not conflict with work?	TRUSTING	Relationship-Based: What can we do together to build authentic relationships?
Confronting: Are we hearing all the ideas within the meeting?	DISAGREEING	Avoiding: How can we gather feedback anonymously?
Linear Time: Which deadlines are nonnegotiable?	SCHEDULING	Flexible Time: What lessons from the past can help us address current challenges?
Principle-First: What fundamental concepts should we wrestle with before action?	PERSUADING	Application-First: Would it be helpful to give practical examples?

Try incorporating a five-minute "culture pulse" before meetings to make culture a regular team topic. Use these questions. If your team has a majority of members from one culture, spend more time asking questions about how to leverage the strengths of cultures with less representation.

3.

FORMING A TEAM CULTURE

Increasing Team Cohesion

Culture eats strategy for breakfast.

–Peter Drucker

"How would you describe your team culture?" I asked Aaron. He gave me a blank stare, as if he wasn't sure what I meant by the question. Then he lit up and pointed to the organizational values posted on the wall. "Everyone has these "WE ARE…" statements posted in their office," he said.

I read them out, pausing after each statement to confirm, "So this describes your team?"

"Well, not exactly…I mean, that is what we aim for." Aaron hesitated, "Our values are aspirational."

I pressed, asking how his team behaved day-by-day. Did they have clear expectations as a team? Had they defined what a good meeting was? I lost count of the number of times Aaron responded with, "It depends."

Forming Your Own Team Culture

We have talked about individual cultural preferences; now, we are talking about forming a team culture. Operating at peak performance requires that team members operate as a team. They must feel safe enough to give it their all without the fear of failure. Creating this atmosphere takes intentionality on the part of the leader. Multicultural teams require even more intentionality and clarity of purpose than monocultural teams. This tool will show you how to form a team culture that will turn diversity into creativity.

WHY IT MATTERS

People affiliate in groups for two reasons, for belonging and to accomplish a common goal. The desire to belong to a group is among the most basic of human needs. We want to be a part of something outside ourselves. We need to feel that we belong before we will take the necessary risks to perform at the highest level.

Clarity of purpose and our drive for belonging is what motivates groups to differentiate themselves. It is a natural process for teams to create behavior patterns and insider language to reinforce ways of working.

Every team naturally develops a team culture, but not every team is intentional about shaping that culture. Norms arise—unspoken rules about how things are done, how decisions are made, and how conflict is dealt with or avoided. Think about team culture on a spectrum from organic to organized.

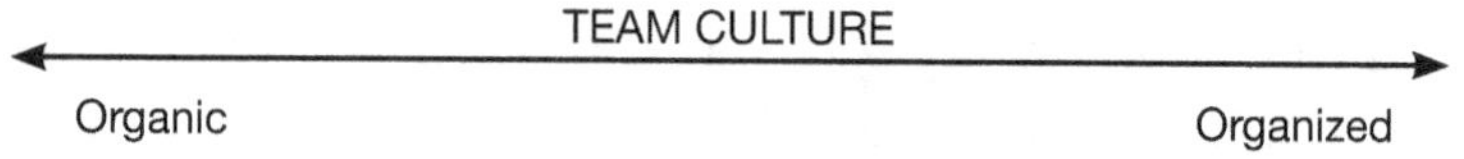

No matter where a team falls on the organic-organized spectrum, it is the leader's job to shape the team culture through an inclusive process. Every hour spent actively shaping a team culture will reap the rewards of team health and, ultimately, team performance.

Some teams, consciously or unconsciously, allow their culture to develop organically. All rules are unspoken. New members slowly figure out how things are done and how decisions are made through trial and error. Nothing is stated openly or written down. Other teams are highly structured. Communication lines and team rules are clearly stated. Where does your team fall on this spectrum? Existing at either extreme comes with risks.

Unspoken assumptions cause confusion.

Multicultural teams require more intentional organization than monocultural teams. They must have a clearer understanding of their common goal to overcome their obvious differences. Clarity is crucial: unspoken assumptions cause confusion. The only way to combat the confusion that arises from cultural differences is to clarify the team's common goal and operating model to achieve it.

HOW IT WORKS

Teams need a reason to exist, a common goal that can only be accomplished by working as a team. Unfortunately, some teams are just thrown together by the organization. They lack any understanding of why they need to work together. In fact, they may feel more productive acting alone. Without a clear purpose for existence, a group is just a group, not a team.

Clarity of purpose is even more critical for multicultural teams. Humans have an unconscious bias to work with people who look like them and think like them. Mixing cultures creates a centrifugal force that threatens to pull teams apart. If it is not 100% clear why the team exists, the team will naturally dissipate. It's easier to operate alone.

The first job of any team leader is to clarify the team's common goal. See Appendix A for more on the importance of team vision. Once the goal is clear, the leader must then shape the team culture—define how they will operate to achieve the goal.

To shape a team's culture, one must understand the basic human need to belong. The desire to belong is what powers human society. We all want to be a part of a group—a family; a team; an organization; a nation. Paradoxically, it is our desire to belong that leads to division. We speak about 'us' and 'them' because of our deep longing to be a part of a group and separate from the masses. Unfortunately, one of the ways to strengthen belonging is by creating distance between insiders and outsiders.

To shape a team's culture, one must understand
the basic human need to belong.

Differentiation is a natural result of forming a group. Imagine a group having a piece of chalk. The first thing they do is draw a circle around their group to show who is in and out. This act of drawing a circle creates a division between those outside and inside. Yet, this division enhances the sense of belonging within the group. Team dynamics are fascinating.

The human practice of drawing circles and creating groups can, at one moment, generate acceptance and safety and, the next, create division and uncertainty. It all depends on how and where the circle is drawn.

Psychological Safety

Amy Edmonson coined the term "psychological safety" to describe when a team knows they are inside the circle. This type of safety is when a team feels comfortable enough to take an interpersonal risk because they experience mutual trust and respect. Team trust is crucial for team health—the first building block of a successful team. Building team trust to ensure psychological safety is the groundwork for forming a team culture. In multicultural teams, trust is more difficult to establish and more fragile.

Psychological safety develops in four stages: inclusion, learning, contributing, and challenging. In his book, *The 4 Stages of Psychological Safety*, Timothy Clark (2020) suggests how a team can progress through each stage.

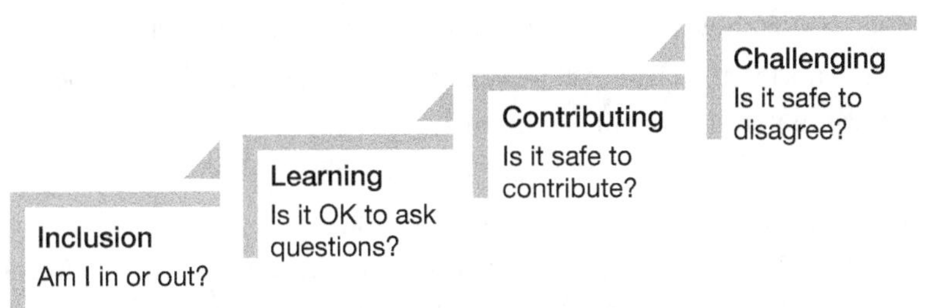

Each member should be able to answer the question at each stage in the affirmative. This is not a one-time exercise. Building a healthy level of trust within your team should be continuous. High-performing teams regularly dedicate time to assessing and cultivating these four stages of safety.

Define Your Team Culture

Value and behavior statements are an excellent tool for cultivating organizational culture, but team culture needs something more detailed. A team needs to define their operating model—how they will behave.

Depending on where your team falls on the organic to organized spectrum, an operating model may be written down or just discussed verbally. Whatever you do, insist on clarity. Do not assume that everyone agrees or knows how the team will function. Assumptions are at the root of cultural misunderstanding.

Assumptions are at the root
of cultural misunderstanding.

So, how do you shape a team culture? Start with a conversation. Use the eight cultural preferences from chapter one and decide *your team's* preference. Move beyond individual opinions; this is the *team* culture. What are the norms and customs that will make your team tick? See Appendix A for more on the forming stage of a team.

This exercise is like the cultural awareness assessment in chapter one, but instead of asking how do *I* think, you ask how do *we* want to think? Remember that the goal is unity, not uniformity. Defining a team culture does not diminish the individual cultures present on the team.

A thoughtfully crafted team culture will create the clarity and safety necessary to bring out the best of diversity. Members should feel able to bring their unique perspectives to the team. The aim is to operate at the highest stages of psychological safety in which team members feel comfortable contributing and challenging others.

During these discussions, it is helpful if the leader is the last to voice their preference. Hierarchical cultures or those who prefer top-down decisions may find it difficult to express opinions that differ from the leader's. Being able to openly discuss these issues is the very reason a team needs to define its culture, but the conversation itself must be entered into humbly and respectfully. Defining a team culture that benefits only a few will erode rather than build trust.

The table below provides guiding questions and tips for each cultural scale.

TEAM CULTURE CONVERSATION	
COMMUNICATING	How will we communicate as a team? Tip: Favor low-context communication. Focus on how you will promote clarity over ambiguity.
EVALUATING	Define 'polite' and 'rude' in our team. Tip: Favor indirect feedback to reinforce safety. Communicate poor performance privately and praise publicly.
LEADING	What types of leadership are encouraged? Tip: Intentionally vary forms of leadership and create opportunities for many to lead.
DECIDING	How will we make decisions? Tip: Agree on the decision-making process before beginning a discussion. Vary the way of deciding according to the situation.

TRUSTING	What will we do to build mutual trust? Tip: Invest time in holistic relationships as part of the team rhythm. Discuss how to value both tasks and relationships.
DISAGREEING	How will we make sure we hear all ideas? Tip: The leader should contribute ideas last. Allow multiple feedback channels. Define a 'good meeting' before the meeting.
SCHEDULING	How do we manage our time? Tip: Create team rules for understanding time— meeting schedules, project deadlines, time zones?
PERSUADING	How should we present or pitch new ideas? Tip: Use smaller, monocultural working groups when efficiency is the goal.

A Note on Language

A team's ability to communicate depends on a common language. Even if every team member speaks English, language might still be a barrier. Ignoring language differences or English competencies will prevent a team from achieving higher levels of psychological safety. As Erin Meyer notes, "Nonnative speakers may become less motivated to contribute, or anxious about their performance evaluations and future career prospects" (2014, p. 87).

Native English speakers should be careful not to assume that English will be used. Assuming the use of any one language can be interpreted as a power play, giving advantage to some while marginalizing others. There is a power dynamic to language within multicultural teams.

Discuss language openly when defining your team culture. Are there times when translation would be beneficial? Simple gestures such as sending out pre-meeting agendas or requiring presentations to be shared in writing for pre-reading can go a long way in enabling members to contribute during the meeting. The benefits of slowing down to allow for diverse contributions far outweigh efficiency.

We Are Always Drawing Circles

When defining a team culture, the aim is to create conditions of belonging and safety. The group is drawing a circle around themselves. As I stated earlier, drawing circles always creates division. Yet, a division is not necessarily a bad thing. Each family creates an identity that is unique to them. They have drawn a circle around their family to clarify who is in and out. Inside the circle, the family belongs and feels safe. The circle changes when a new member joins the family through marriage or having a child.

Some multicultural teams fail to develop an identity because they hesitate to draw a circle. They never define their team culture for fear of showing favoritism or excluding those outside the team. Yet, without a circle, there is no belonging or safety. The way to avoid excluding or showing favoritism is not to have no circle: it is to draw more circles, larger circles.

---

*Drawing a circle around a team
creates an identity unique to that team.*

Humans are always drawing circles. So, if someone feels excluded, draw a bigger circle. Get the whole team involved in drawing their own team circle.

WHAT TO DO NEXT

If you've never fully defined your team culture, I suggest the following team exercise. Set aside enough time separate from your normal meeting rhythm to ensure that regular business topics do not creep into the discussion. Ideally, make this part of a team-building retreat. This exercise could immediately follow the team discussions suggested in the first two chapters, but it could easily be a separate conversation.

Ensure that the entire team starts from a place of safety. If trust or mutual respect is lacking on your team, address those before attempting this exercise. Remember, you are drawing a circle as a team, so if people already feel divided, an exercise intended to unite could end up causing more division.

Team Circle Exercise

Begin by explaining the concepts in this chapter or ask team members to review the material before coming together. Have everyone draw a line down the middle of a piece of paper. On one side, have them represent the "team circle" as it is today—a visual depiction of the current state of the team's culture. How defined is the circle? Is it whole or broken? On the other side, ask them to draw what they *want* the team to look like. Encourage creativity—what would benefit the team's sense of belonging, trust, and safety? Let them draw something inside both circles if they wish. Ask each one to briefly share their pictures to the group.

Next, develop a draft team charter. You may want to call it something else that better reflects your team: agreement, playbook, way of working, TOR, behavior statements, team rules, etc. The idea is to clarify your team culture together and then write it down.

Use the **Team Culture Conversation** questions given earlier in this chapter to go through all eight cultural preferences. Decide ahead of time how you will ensure that everyone's thoughts are heard, especially from those who may be less assertive. Aim to end with a brief document of five to eight norms or customs that define your team.

Finally, develop visual cues that symbolize what your team has decided. Choose words, symbols, or pictures that are unique to your team. These will act as reminders of the shared norms. Decide what is appropriate in your context, but do not dismiss the idea of creating visual reminders. It is part of drawing your circle, and it is fun! Commit to revisiting this team culture document regularly—at least annually—or when a new team member joins.

4.

RESOLVING CROSS-CULTURAL CONFLICT

Healthy Debate and Psychological Safety

Peace cannot be kept by force.
It can only be achieved by understanding.

–Albert Einstein

Conflict can be healthy; teams should encourage disagreement. In fact, the absence of conflict is a red flag indicating that the team culture may not allow different opinions. So, how can a leader facilitate healthy debate and help resolve disputes? There are many books on conflict resolution. Rather than attempting to summarize all of them in this chapter, I will focus our discussion on cross-cultural conflict.

During my first few years of working in a multicultural team, I had a team member who I quickly labeled as my enemy. Bisrat seemed to fight me every chance he got. No matter the issue, I could count on him to be on the opposite side. We disagreed about everything.

One day, as I was complaining about Bisrat, a colleague asked me how I thought Bisrat felt about me. The question threw me off, but I eventually began to imagine the situation from Bisrat's perspective. Maybe *I* was the enemy who was fighting *him* at every turn. I had never sought to really understand his cultural perspective. From then on, I became curious rather than judgmental. Our relationship changed instantly. We still disagreed, but he became a trusted colleague rather than an enemy.

In multicultural teams, cultural differences are often at the core of conflicts. Simply recognizing the underlying cultural motivations is a good start, and sometimes that is enough. Other times, you need more. The first three chapters were about noticing cultural assumptions and addressing those differences. This chapter is about facing cultural conflict head-on.

WHY IT MATTERS

When dealing with conflict, the leader must avoid becoming the sole mediator between cultures. A leader often has more experience working with other cultures or feels like maybe they *should* have more experience. If the leader does feel comfortable stepping into culturally tense situations, there is a danger that the team will become dependent on the leader being a mediator.

Leaders with high cross-cultural aptitude run the risk of creating team dependency. A better long-term strategy is empowerment. In a healthy team, everyone learns tools for respectful disagreement and encourages all members to reach higher levels of cultural adaptation.

I cannot stress this enough. Too many leaders think they are doing the team a service by stepping in and resolving cross-cultural conflict. Unfortunately, a growth opportunity is missed by failing to teach the group. High-performing teams do not rely on the leader to come to the rescue. They proactively seek resolutions among themselves.

Remember that conflict is a part of a healthy team. Whenever people care about the outcome, there should be different opinions and disagreements. The absence of conflict is a red flag signaling a lack of safety within the team. Therefore, the entire team needs to learn what healthy conflict looks like and what to do when the battle changes from healthy to unhealthy.

HOW IT WORKS

Simply taking the time to define terms can resolve most human conflicts.

While working in Ethiopia, I overheard an argument between two team members. Faith, an American, was clearly troubled about something, so Haile, an Ethiopian, said with fatherly composure, "Faith, stop thinking. You are thinking too much."

Faith, somewhat bewildered, retorted, "Why should I stop thinking? This issue is important." To which Haile repeated, "Yes, but do not think so much." Faith's frustration rose, "But I *want* to think. This is *important*!"

Their voices steadily rose until they were a distraction to everyone in the room. Obviously, they both had very different definitions of "thinking." Haile was telling Faith not to worry. Faith thought he was being dismissive and demeaning, implying that she should not reflect on the situation or strategize a solution. When they finally clarified their words, they laughed it off, allowing everyone to get back to work.

Build a Foundation of Trust

The first three chapters of this book have given you tools to help your team clarify their words. The eight cultural preference scales provide a common language, a way to talk about the underlying cultural assumptions that are often at the root of conflicts large and small. Identifying the most significant gaps between team members' preferences gives your team a way to talk about differences in a productive manner. Too often, conflict is simply a matter of lacking common terminology.

Most conflict can be resolved
by defining our terms.

However, using the right words does nothing if trust is lacking. Trust is the foundation of a team. Anything that is built upon a shaky foundation eventually crumbles. Teams that fail to address a lack of trust fall apart or, worse, get stuck in mediocrity.

Trust is an overarching theme throughout this book that should not be taken for granted. Trust is critical for all teams, but even more so in multicultural teams because it takes more time to develop. Different cultures establish trust differently and at different paces.

Look back at where your team falls on the TRUSTING scale between tasks and relationships. A multicultural team must intentionally work on building connections at both ends of this spectrum. Team members need to understand the importance of trusting with tasks (being reliable) and trusting relationally (being vulnerable).

Personal History Exercise

One simple exercise to build trust, suggested by Patrick Lencioni (2012), is to have teams share their personal histories. Set aside enough time to allow at least 10-15 minutes per team member. Starting with the leader, give each member a chance to tell their story. Start with the basics of where you were born and family size. Then share the challenges you faced growing up that shaped who you are today.

I recommend informing the team of this exercise a few days in advance. If language is an issue, give them the option of writing down their stories ahead of time and even offer to let someone else read them to the group. Alternatively, use an interview format. Hand out a list of questions in pairs, and have them take turns interviewing each other one-on-one, but in front of the group.

The goal is to allow space for each person to share something from their background that they feel will help the team understand who they are and why they work the way they do. It may sound simple, but even in groups that have been together for years, this exercise can be foundational for building trust.

Skilling Up All Team Members

Pay attention to where your team falls on the DISAGREEING scale between confronting and avoiding. Individuals have different preferences for dealing with conflict, so you should have already clarified what disagreeing looks like in your team.

So, what do you do when you're in the middle of a conflict? Healthy conflict resolution takes practice. The good news is that you can use the same tools while in the middle of a conflict as you do when you are just talking about disagreeing. Don't wait until a problem arises. Skill up your team now. Try these simple tips to begin incorporating conflict resolution into your everyday discussions.

- **Frame disagreements as opportunities for innovation.** Verbally state your belief that differences are to be leveraged as strengths, not avoided as obstacles. Erin Meyer says, "Sometimes just a few words of explanation framing your behavior can make all the difference in how your actions are perceived" (2014, p. 218).

- **Designate a devil's advocate.** Assign someone the task of arguing the opposite side even if they do not personally hold this view. This is a good exercise in creative thinking, and it relieves the tension if someone else actually does have that view but is unwilling to speak up.

- **Hold a meeting before the meeting.** If you foresee disagreement, meet with members one-on-one beforehand. Let them know you look forward to hearing all the ideas, but only if the discussion remains constructive. You might even agree on a secret signal between you that can be used to pause the conversation in the event that emotions run too high.

- **Learn as a team.** Create a habit of learning conflict resolutions skills as a team. Read a book together to increase your shared language. There are many good ones. If you don't know where to start, grab several copies of *Crucial Conversations* (Patterson et al., 2012) and read through it together one chapter at a time.

Setting the Team Up for Success

Resolve the small things before they become big things. If conflicts are ignored, they fester and grow. This is particularly true in multicultural teams when differences stem from misunderstandings based on assumptions we are often unaware of. Below are three strategies for dealing with larger issues that simply eliminating misunderstanding cannot always resolve.

- **Escalate one level up.** All team members should learn and practice conflict resolution, but sometimes a mediator is required. Set expectations for when it is appropriate to use the team leader as a mediator versus someone else within the team or a third party. From which culture should the mediator come? When is it appropriate to involve the next level up (the leader's supervisor)? What will be the mediator's role? It is best to discuss and agree upon these questions before an issue arises, not in the middle of a conflict.

- **Structure the team for success.** Consider that conflict might be due to the wrong team structure. Make sure work is assigned appropriately to the right group of people. Projects that require quick decisions might be better suited to individuals or small working groups. Allow group work to remain within one culture if efficiency is critical. Leverage diversity if creativity is prioritized.
- **Exit IS an option.** I have seen teams disintegrate due to a leader's unwillingness to remove a problem employee. Do not hesitate to remove a team member if all other options have failed. When a leader recognizes a problem but fails to act, the leader's inaction becomes the problem.

WHAT TO DO NEXT

This chapter has several practical suggestions for building your leadership muscle in conflict resolution. Just pick one idea and implement it. Learn the concept for yourself, and then teach it to your team.

Conflicts fester due to inaction. Even if your team culture leans toward avoidance, inaction should not be an option. Multicultural teams that fail to build conflict resolution skills will never reach high performance. All cultures can learn ways to deal with conflict that still respect cultural preferences.

Team Self-Observation

Learning begins with reflection. Before your team can improve its conflict resolution skills, it must first gain individual and group awareness on how each member prefers to deal with conflict. One tool is the well-known Intercultural Conflict Style (ICS) inventory (Hammer, 2009). Alternatively, try this simple exercise to broach the subject and get the conversation started.

Set up a phone or laptop camera to capture the faces of each team member in the room. Give the team a controversial topic to discuss that has nothing to do with your work—something that is sure to create a good discussion but is not personal. Some ideas:

- Which make better pets: dogs or cats?
- Is social media good or bad for society?
- Is lying always wrong?
- Should sugar be regulated like a drug?

You can assign who will argue which side or leave it up to them depending on the personalities present in your team. The goal is to create a lively discussion on film for 5-10 minutes.

Now re-watch the interaction and ask each team member to comment on what they see. Pause the video and allow individuals to describe what they were feeling at that moment. Observe changes in posture, facial expressions, or tone of voice.

Use the video to start a conversation about HOW you disagree. What do you want to do more of or less of? Decide as a team what types of behaviors to encourage and how to build your conflict resolution skills.

5.

CREATING AN INTERCULTURAL CLIMATE

Organizational Transformation

If you want to go fast, go alone.
If you want to go far, go together.

–African proverb

Most of my career has been spent leading teams outside of my passport country. As a leader of multicultural teams, I was confronted with stark differences in assumptions and preferences daily. However, my greatest source of frustration was often communication with the head office in my home country.

Messages from the head office in the United States often contained American idioms, inside jokes, or sarcasm that didn't translate well. I was asked to explain cultural references mentioned without any context in meetings. The head office was unaware of the confusion they caused for other cultures. I felt I constantly had to play the role of cultural interpreter.

Repackaging messages coming from the head office to my team and then doing the same in reverse meant that I was a communication bottleneck. It took too much of my time and, I was burning out. Acting as a cultural translator between teams did not get at the root cause of the issue. I was slowing everything down.

While complaining about the situation, my coach asked, "Andrew, how much influence do you have at the enterprise level? Strategic leaders lead beyond just their team; they impact the entire organization."

I came away from that coaching conversation with an expanded vision and a broader understanding of my role. During the next two years, I took every opportunity to promote cultural awareness within the organization. I became a champion of cross-cultural training, helping those at the head office understand our global teams and supporting our international teams so that they could better relate to the head office culture.

Strategic leaders lead beyond just their team;
they impact the entire organization.

Change certainly did not happen overnight, and I was not acting alone, but the results were transformational. The organization's culture began to resemble an intercultural climate that fostered high-performing multicultural teams. This chapter presents tools for transforming your organization into a space for multicultural teams to flourish.

WHY IT MATTERS

One high-performing multicultural team is a powerful force, but many multicultural teams change the whole organization. The trajectory shifts when members of a multicultural team begin leading multicultural teams of their own. Cascading influence can become a flywheel that propels an organization forward.

Multicultural teams thrive in an intercultural environment. Like trees, they need the right combination of soil, sun, water, and favorable competition. Everyone appreciates the shade that trees provide, but not everyone takes the initiative to plant a tree. Even fewer people take the time to tend to the soil to help a new tree grow. Yet, we all reap the benefits of shade. Trees can transform a landscape.

Similarly, multicultural teams can transform your organization, but they need to be planted in a friendly environment—an intercultural climate—to thrive. Many global organizations unknowingly stifle such teams by allowing one culture to dominate—that of HQ.

An organization must intentionally foster interculturalism; it does not happen automatically. It always amazes me how many leaders think that company culture is just what it is and cannot be changed. Leaders who fail to shape company culture overlook one of their greatest sources of influence. Culture shaping is the groundwork of organizational transformation.

Leaders who fail to shape company culture overlook their greatest source of influence.

Much has been written about the elusive concept of organizational transformation. It is more than just change; it is becoming adaptable. We live in a world of volatility, uncertainty, complexity, and ambiguity. The business world even has an acronym for these realities: VUCA (volatile, uncertain, complex, and ambiguous).

Any organization that fails to change will inevitably stagnate. Fostering an intercultural climate liberates teams to do what they are meant to do—the vital work of innovating, solving problems, and thinking outside of the box. Organizational transformation happens when multicultural teams thrive rather than fight to survive.

HOW IT WORKS

The first four tools were about using cultural diversity to achieve high performance by engraining multiculturalism into the team. This last tool does the same at the organizational level by creating an intercultural climate.

So, what is an intercultural climate? What characterizes this environment that breathes life into multicultural teams and allows them to multiply? Answer: diversity, inclusion, and belonging.

Culture is just one form of diversity, but understanding diversity is critical for today's strategic leaders. In the introduction, we recommended Anand's *Leading Global Diversity, Equity, and Inclusion* (2021). Pick up a copy now and read it. You will thank me later. The main takeaway is that global organizations often employ a single-culture approach when implementing DEI efforts. These efforts inevitably fail if the organization has not developed an intercultural climate first.

Yet, to create an intercultural climate, we must recognize that diversity alone has no value. Only when coupled with inclusion and belonging do we begin to realize diversity's benefits.

Diversity is a fact, a condition. Inclusion and belonging are choices and actions. Simply putting different cultures together in an organization does not unleash creative potential. These are just the conditions. Choices and actions are required to foster inclusion and encourage belonging. Diversity, inclusion, and belonging are necessary parts of an intercultural climate.

Cultural Diversity

An intercultural climate celebrates individual cultures present within an organization while simultaneously creating one common organizational culture. Leadership is often about paradoxes or apparent contradictions where views seem opposite, but both are true. Employees need to feel both celebrated individually and unified as a group The paradox is that a leader strengthens collective identity by recognizing and highlighting individual identities.

The first step to cultural diversity is hiring and promoting people from diverse cultures. Do a quick inventory of your organization. Is one culture overrepresented in leadership? Is one culture completely absent? Many organizations claim to want to build an intercultural climate but get stuck on this first step.

When I ask leaders about their organization's cultural diversity, the conversation often goes something like this:

HQ leader: 90% of our workforce is located outside the U.S. We operate in 15 different languages across 20 countries.

Me: So, how many nationalities are represented on your board of directors?

HQ leader: *Silence.*

Me: How do you ensure major decisions about the organization's strategic direction receive input from all cultural perspectives?

HQ leader: *Blank stares.*

Organizational transformation does not happen overnight. It starts with an idea that leads to a robust debate and then to a decision that is then communicated and reworked based on feedback and repeated until everyone is committed (or at least not resistant).

Remember that with today's virtual tools, building culturally diverse leadership does not have to mean relocating leaders to all sit in one office. Start with changing who is in the room or who joins on a screen. Start with a simple commitment to intentionally shift the representation, authority, and eventually the decision-making power away from one dominant culture.

Cultural Inclusion

If diversity alone is not enough, how do we ensure inclusion? The secret to cultural inclusion lies in one word: curiosity. Can the leaders of your organization effectively leverage all cultural perspectives? Intercultural climates elevate learning above expertise and knowing.

Overconfidence in expertise is the opposite of curiosity. When people feel that they either know it all or are expected to know it all, they exclude new ideas rather than welcome them. The same is true of culture. Cultural inclusion starts with a climate of curiosity.

I recommend that organizations train all levels in practical tools to increase curiosity in daily interactions. Listing "learning" or "curiosity" as corporate values is not enough. Train leaders in humble inquiry. There are many resources available that teach this concept. One way I recommend encouraging humble inquiry is through teaching coaching skills.

Cultural inclusion starts
with a climate of curiosity.

Coaching is all about being curious and asking questions. If done appropriately, it transcends cultural differences. I describe coaching as answering the question, "Where do you want to go, and how can I help you get there?" Imagine what would happen in your organization if leaders at all levels were given basic coaching skills with the expectation of putting them into practice supervising, leading teams, and facilitating meetings.

Sometimes coaching skills are taught in isolation. Leaders learn active listening, how to ask clarifying questions, or how to co-create an action plan. But when taught together in the context of cultural inclusion, these skills give leaders the tools to create an environment of curiosity that fosters innovation and transformation. An organization that teaches coaching as a leadership skill lays the groundwork for cultural inclusion.

For more information on coaching and incorporating humble inquiry into your organizational culture, see *Coaching: The First Five Tools for Strategic Leaders* from the ClarionToolBox Series.

Cultural Belonging

The final element of creating an intercultural climate is belonging. Cultural belonging is present when employees feel like they are a part of the organizational culture as a whole. Are the organization's mission, vision, and values culturally relevant? Is the strategic narrative, the grand story of where the organization came from and where it is headed, culturally relevant? Or was it shaped exclusively within the dominant culture and imposed upon the minority cultures? These may be difficult questions, but they are nonetheless critical to ask.

Cultural belonging begins with engagement. Individuals and teams from across cultures need a way to engage with one another regularly. Most organizations have a mixture of multicultural teams and mono-cultural teams. But all employees should have the opportunity to engage cross-culturally, even if not in a formal group. Organizations should foster engagement outside of teams.

Cross-cultural team interactions can be both intentional and organic. But if leaders leave cultural engagement to chance, interactions will be concentrated around certain individuals. Cultural belonging comes out of an organizational-wide effort to increase cross-cultural engagement at all levels.

---

*From day one, all employees should know
that they are joining a global team.*

Increasing engagement means more than just expanding the travel budget. Flying individuals around for face-to-face interaction is valuable but is not the only way to engage. One practical suggestion is to include cultural awareness training in orientation materials. Rather than offering a primer on cross-cultural engagement before an employee's first international trip, include this as part of every staff member's introduction to the organization. From day one, all employees should feel they are joining a global team and will be expected to engage cross-culturally.

Cultural awareness should also be part of an organization's performance evaluation process. Determining who gets promoted or is given a leadership role reveals an organization's values. If cultural belonging is held as a value, this should be reflected in how performance is evaluated. Promote those who demonstrate cultural sensitivity and actively seek opportunities to engage globally. Doing so will lay the foundation for an intercultural climate.

WHAT TO DO NEXT

Begin with an honest evaluation of where your organization is today. Use the table below as an assessment. Adapt it to fit your specific context.

Intercultural Climate Assessment	Where are we today?					How can we move up one level?
	Ignore	Recognize	Adapt	Integrate	Leverage	
	1	2	3	4	5	
Organizational Identity						
Mission, Vision, & Values are culturally relevant and inclusive						
Cross-cultural training is a part of orientation and onboarding at all levels						
Cultural awareness is incorperated into all performance evaluations						
Global Communication						
Organizational communication is culturally sensitive (e-mail, collaboration platforms, all-staff updates)						

Team meeting rhythms consider cultural preferences and global time zones							
Language barriers are addressed openly to ensure global participation							
Opportunites for cross-cultural engagement are present across all teams and locations							
Leadership and Decision-making							
The Board of Directors reflects the organization's cultural diversity							
The Executive Team reflects the organization's cultural diversity							
Cultural perspectives are considered before making major decisions							
Cultural awareness is a part of promotion decisions and leadership appointments							
Leadership training includes cultural curiosity (coaching, humble inquiry, inclusion)							

For each item on the assessment, ask the question, "What would it take to move up one level?" Remember, the goal is progress, not perfection. Focus on one or two areas where the next steps are clear and achievable.

CONCLUSION

The more we learn,
the more questions we have.

Judge a man by his questions
rather than his answers.

–Voltaire

In the preface, I introduced you to my friend Ishmael, a Fulani herdsman living with his family on the edge of the Sahara Desert. Ishmael taught me more about culture than any book or workshop ever could. He taught me to be curious; he taught me the importance of asking questions.

One evening, while gazing at the night sky, he asked me to share some sayings in English. Proverbs were very significant in his culture, so he often asked for sayings. At that particular moment, I was struck by how small the world was. So, I explained to him how in English, we often say it's a small world. It caught me off guard when he began laughing out loud. He said that was ridiculous. I felt myself getting defensive and wanting to explain why and when it was appropriate to speak of the world being small.

But then I became curious. I wanted to know what Ishmael found so funny. He looked up at the night sky and said, "Andrew, the world is *huge*."

He was absolutely right. The world is huge. It is full of diversity, and when we try to take it all in, the only appropriate response is wonder.

Curiosity and Questions

Leading multicultural teams takes humility, intentionality, and persistence, but most of all, it takes the willingness to be curious and ask questions. Start by humbly recognizing where you are today, then intentionally plan the next steps. Be persistent. Recognize that moving from chaos to clarity doesn't happen overnight. I hope these first five tools are only the beginning of a life-long journey for you, your team, and your organization.

Appendix A:

Managing High-Performance Teams

There are many excellent books on leading teams. The second book in the ClarionToolBox Series, *Building Strategic Organizations,* is a great place to start.

Strategic leaders clarify a team's mission, vision, and values; summarize where the team is going and how to get there in a few high-level objectives; and execute projects that will lead the team in the right direction, measuring progress along the way. These tasks are equally vital for multicultural teams, but their need for clarity is even higher.

Every team needs a regular rhythm for discussing each level of strategic altitude: vision, strategy, and tactical. A common mistake is to mix all three altitudes in one meeting. The resulting confusion inevitably means that tactical, to-do lists take up most meetings and suck the energy out of the team. No one wants to sit around a table for an hour hearing mundane updates. The team leader is responsible for setting a meeting rhythm and clarifying the altitude for each meeting.

Meeting Type	Meeting Purpose	Duration & Frequency
Visionary	Where are we going?	Full day: Quarterly or Semi-annually
Strategic	How can we get there?	1-2 hours: Monthly or Bi-weekly
Tactical	What needs to be done?	15min max: Weekly or even Daily

I recommend frequent but short "update meetings" for tactical discussions. Some call these huddles, stand-up meetings, or a daily scrum. The important thing is that they are brief, frequent, and focused only on tasks. If strategic questions are raised, take note of them, add them to the agenda for the next strategic meeting, or if urgent, schedule an ad hoc meeting to address only that issue. Adhering to a strict time limit (usually less than 15 minutes) helps keep everyone focused at the tactical level.

---

*Mediocre teams lack the discipline
to dedicate time to vision-level thinking.*

Focus strategic meetings around measuring progress. In *Building Strategic Organizations,* we provide a template for a Monthly Strategy Review. Use this meeting to go through your team's indicators. Each objective should have a measure that is either green (on track), yellow (needs attention), or red (critically behind). Again, keep this meeting focused on the strategic level. If tactical issues are raised, remind the team that the meeting is about evaluating progress toward the strategic objectives. Strategic meetings are not the time to give updates or list detailed actions.

Visionary level meetings ask the question, where are we going? Set aside dedicated vision time, at minimum every year, but quarterly is better. These meetings are when the team reevaluates its strategic objectives. Are we headed in the right direction? What is the most important thing to be focusing on this year? Wrestling with these big questions is one of the most rewarding aspects of being a part of a high-performance team, but it takes intentionality. Mediocre teams lack the discipline needed to dedicate time to vision-level thinking.

Five Behaviors of a Cohesive Team

Patrick Lencioni (2012) uses five levels to describe a cohesive team. Each level is foundational to the one above it; all five are necessary to achieve high performance.

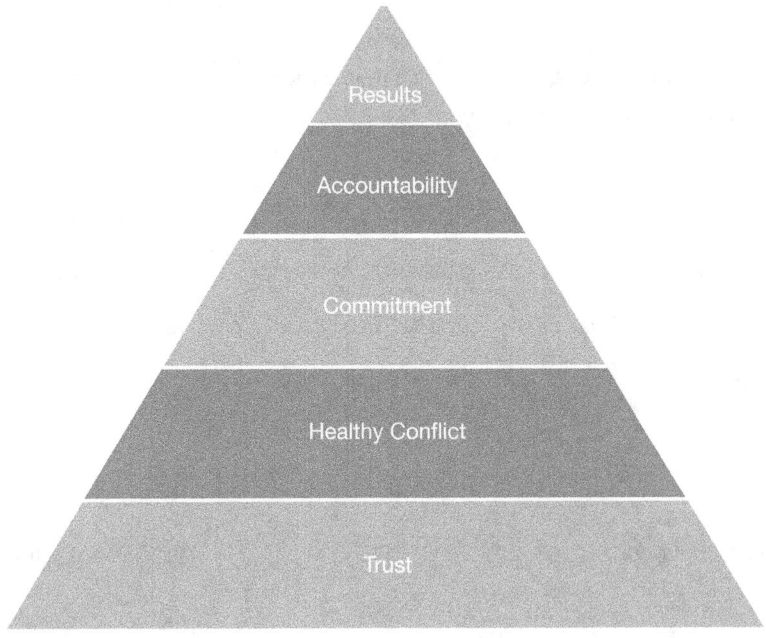

I use Lencioni's pyramid with the teams I work with and find that it always generates a lively discussion. With multicultural teams, it is worthwhile to spend extra time defining each level. Let the team come up with examples of both dysfunction and high-performance for each of the five behaviors.

Appendix B:

Cultural Assessments

As described in chapter one, you can use the example below to conduct a cultural assessment with your team.

Cultural Differences		
Low context	COMMUNICATING	High Context
Direct Negative Feedback	EVALUATING	Indirect Negative Feedback
Egalitarian	LEADING	Hierarchical
Consensual	DECIDING	Top Down
Task-Based	TRUSTING	Relationship Based
Confrontational	DISAGREEING	Avoid Confrontation
Linear Time	SCHEDULING	Flexible Time
Principles First	PERSUADING	Applications First

A thorough understanding of each side of the spectrum is key to accurately assessing one's culture. If teams do not fully understand the descriptions of each cultural preference, they will have difficulty self-identifying where their culture falls on each line.

A great way to check how well your team understands each cultural preference is to check your assessment against the research. Country mapping tools are available at www.erinmeyer.com. You can input multiple cultures and map where they fall on each of the eight scales for a small fee. These positions are based on research and can be very enlightening, especially for teams that may not understand their culture's relative position compared to others. This tool makes it easy to highlight the widest cultural gaps present on your team.

Hofstede's Cultural Dimensions

Alternatively, use the free tool for comparing countries found at https://www.hofstede-insights.com/country-comparison/germany,the-usa/. This tool uses Hofstede's six dimensions: Power Distance, Individualism, Masculinity, Uncertainty Avoidance, Long Term Orientation, and Indulgence. While these do not precisely correlate with Myer's eight scales, they are an excellent way to understand the significant differences between national cultures.

Intercultural Development Inventory

One of the best assessments for measuring cultural awareness is the Intercultural Development Inventory (IDI). This tool measures an individual's level of cultural competence. It can be found at https://idiinventory.com/

Appendix C:

Identifying with Multiple Cultures

Much of this book is written with the assumption that leaders and their teams identify with one primary national culture. While this is true for most individuals, there are a growing number of people who struggle to identify with only one culture. They may have grown up outside of their home country, spent significant periods emersed in a culture other than that of their parents, or have a family life that mixes more than one culture. Children of military families or international workers are often called third culture kids (TCKs). These individuals may assess their preferences differently.

Third culture kids or adults may struggle to articulate their cultural preferences. They likely have developed a global identity that incorporates a wide range of acceptable behavior. No one should feel constrained or forced to fit into a specific set of expectations. Remember that every individual is unique, and cultural preferences are only helpful in uncovering national-level assumptions.

If you or others on your team identify with multiple cultures, feel free to include several national cultures for one individual. For example, if a German manager spent their childhood living in Thailand, but has been working in the US for the past decade, include all three cultures on the scale.

Every individual has multiple layers of identity, and viewing each through cultural preferences is a valuable exercise. Walt Whitman famously said, "Do I contradict myself? Very well, then, I contradict myself; I am large. I contain multitudes."

About the Authors

Andrew Hoskins has led and taught multicultural teams for the past two decades. He spent the first 17 years of his career living and working across multiple countries in Africa: Niger, Mali, Ethiopia, Liberia, and Uganda. He is currently the Vice President of International Programs for The Exodus Road, a nonprofit fighting to disrupt global human trafficking.

Andrew is currently completing a DBA at Trevecca Nazarene University. He holds an MA in International Development from the University of South Carolina. He is an Associate Certified Coach (ACC) through the International Coaching Federation (ICF), and a Proci Certified Change Management Practitioner.

Rick Mann, PhD, is the Managing Director of ClarionStrategy, a consulting firm that seeks to build strategic leaders and organizations through coaching, consulting, and courses. He has served in a number of leadership roles across a variety of industries. He also currently serves as Professor of Leadership and Strategy as well as Program Director for the MBA and DBA programs at Trevecca Nazarene University. In the past, he has served as President and Provost of Crown College (MN), a program director in Asia, an executive coach, and a coaching trainer. His areas of interest and expertise begin with a passion for helping leaders and organizations to access and leverage the best thinking in strategy-making and leadership development today.

Rick has an MDiv from Ambrose University (Canada) in cross-cultural studies, an MBA from the University of Minnesota, and an MA and PhD in language, learning, and culture from Ohio State University. He is an Associate Certified Coach through the International Coaching Federation (ICF).

References

Anand, R. (2021). *Leading global diversity, equity, and inclusion: A guide for systemic change in multinational organizations.* Berrett-Koehler Publishers.

Brett, J., Behfar, K., & Kern, M. C. (2006). Managing multicultural teams. *Harvard Business Review, 84*(11), 84–91.

Clark, T.R., (2020). *The 4 stages of psychological safety: Defining the path to inclusion and innovation.* Berrett-Koehler Publishers.

Edmonson, A.C., (2012). *Teaming: How organizations learn, innovate, and compete in the knowledge economy.* John Wiley & Sons.

Giannakoulias, D. (2020). shifting our focus: Discovering deep diversity. *Organization Development Review, 52*(4), 72–74.

Hajro, A., Gibson, C. B., & Pudelko, M. (2017). Knowledge exchange processes in multicultural teams: Linking organizational diversity climates to teams' effectiveness. *Academy of Management Journal, 60*(1), 345–372.

Hammer, M. R. (2009). Solving problems and resolving conflict using the intercultural conflict style model and inventory. *Contemporary leadership and intercultural competence: Exploring the cross-cultural dynamics within organizations,* 219-232.

Henry, T. (2013). *The accidental creative: How to be brilliant at a moment's notice.* Penguin.

Hofstede, G., Hofstede, G.J., & Minkov, M. (2005). *Cultures and organizations: Software of the mind* (Vol. 2). McGraw-Hill.

Javidan, M. (2013). Comments on the Interview: Competencies required for working across borders and managing multicultural teams. *Academy of Management Learning & Education, 12*(3), 506–508.

Lee, Y.-T., Masuda, A. D., Fu, X., & Reiche, B. S. (2018). Navigating between home, host, and global: Consequences of multicultural team members' identity configurations. *Academy of Management Discoveries, 4*(2), 180–201.

Lencioni, P. (2012). *The advantage: Why organizational health trumps everything else in business.* Jossey-Bass.

Meyer, E. (2014). *The culture map: Breaking through the invisible boundaries of global business.* PublicAffairs.

Molinsky, A., & Gundling, E. (2016). How to build trust on your cross-cultural team. *Harvard Business Review Digital Articles*, 2–5. https://hbr.org/2016/06/how-to-build-trust-on-your-cross-cultural-team

Patterson, K., Grenny, J., McMillan, R., & Switzler, A. (2012). *Crucial conversations: Tools for talking when stakes are high.* McGraw-Hill Education.

Rosinski, P. (2003). *Coaching across cultures: New tools for leveraging national, corporate & professional differences.* Nicholas Brealey International.

www.ingramcontent.com/pod-product-compliance
Lightning Source LLC
Chambersburg PA
CBHW061346140726
47997CB00003B/1078